Brimming with creative inspiration, how-to projects, and useful information to enrich your everyday life, Quarto Knows is a favorite destination for those pursuing their interests and passions. Visit our site and dig deeper with our books into your area of interest: Quarto Creates, Quarto Cooks, Quarto Homes, Quarto Lives, Quarto Drives, Quarto Explores, Quarto Gifts, or Quarto Kids.

© 2017 Quarto Publishing Group USA Inc.
Text © 2017 Cornelia Maude Spelman

First Published in 2017 by Seagrass Press, an imprint of The Quarto Group.
6 Orchard Road, Suite 100, Lake Forest, CA 92630, USA.
T (949) 380-7510 **F** (949) 380-7575 **www.QuartoKnows.com**

Seagrass Press titles are also available at discount for retail, wholesale, promotional, and bulk purchase. For details, contact the Special Sales Manager by email at specialsales@quarto.com or by mail at The Quarto Group, Attn: Special Sales Manager, 401 Second Avenue North, Suite 310, Minneapolis, MN 55401 USA.

ISBN: 978-1-63322-384-4

Design: Nick Tiemersma
Editor: Bernette Ford

Printed in China

10 9 8 7 6 5 4 3 2 1

To all the children "Everywhere!"
—CMS

To Andrew. You always believed this would happen for me.
—AM

Everybody's somewhere,
Where are you?

I'm right here,
I'm somebody, too.

Some are in the country,
Some are in the town.

Everybody's somewhere,
Up or down.

Each of us is somewhere
Here or there.

Each of us is someone
In our own somewhere.

You are there, somewhere,
I am right here.
Which of us is far away?
Which of us is near?

Somebody is flying,

Someone's in a car.

Everywhere there's someone
Underneath a star.

If only you came here,
Or I could just go there,

Then we could be together
In our own somewhere.

Someone's in
the treetops.

Someone's on the ground.

Someone's in a marathon,
Running all around.

Somebody's at home,
Someone's gone away.

I'm feeling very happy
When my someone comes to stay.

Everywhere there's someone,
Maybe someone tall.
Somewhere else there's
Somebody awfully small.

Somebody is nowhere!
How could that be?
Nowhere is somewhere
If you ask me.

Someone's at a party.
Someone is in bed.

Each of us is somewhere,
If only in our head.

Somebody's at Grandma's,
Having honey tea.

Somebody is reading this...